THE LONG MARCH

Denis Hoy

Published by: Edmonton Hundred Historical Society
ISBN 0 902922 58 0

PREFACE

This book is published by Edmonton Hundred Historical Society in memory of Denis Hoy. It has been edited by J.Burnby. Denis was born in Wood Green and apart from the time covered in this book was always a local resident. He was a long time member of the society and a long term member of the committee. He served in a number of posts from 1972 onwards - as meetings secretary, as treasurer, as publicity organiser, and as representative to numerous kindred societies. His working life was spent in insurance, he was meticulous in detail and his advice in financial matters was freely given and pertinent.
We remember Denis with high regard and grateful thanks.

Betty Smith - Chairman

Denis L Hoy

REMINDERS

The sudden sweetness of the rose,
The tang of tar and wood fires smoke,
The rustling leaves, when autumn's breeze
From cherry trees removes their cloak,
The lash of rain against my face,
The pop of chestnuts on the fire,
The tender touch of lips so sweet,
The vibrant strumming of the lyre,
Of those I've loved in bygone days,
These scents, these sounds, these touches all
Remind me and yet more amaze
That life goes on beyond the wall,
That holds me here whilst I await
With patience small the open gate.

Denis L Hoy - October 1940.

THE LONG MARCH

Elblin

Marien-
Werder

Thorn

R. Vistula

Linde

Neu-Stettin

POLAND

BALTIC
SEA

Stettin

R. Oder

Usedom
Island

Wollin
Island

BERLIN

Greifswald

Demmin

Malchin

Waren

GERMANY

Parchin

R. Elbe

Hamburg

Harz
Mountains

Lünberger
Heide

Celle

Hildesheim

Einbeck

4

MY LAST DAYS OF LIBERTY.

"History is being made and the QVRs' are not taking part", said Lance Corporal Norris.[1] We were lying reasonable comfort on makeshift beds of blankets on mattresses of flour sacks in the Company Office-cum-Stores which was serving as our bedroom. In happier times this apartment was a granary over a pigsty in which pigs still grunted contentedly that night. The place was a farm close to Kennington, near Ashford, Kent.

I thought Norris, the Company Clerk, somewhat pompous, and anyway I had no wish "to make history". The countryside that Spring was at its most delightful green, especially in the 'Garden of England'.Rumour had it, that after being pitchforked out of our winter quarters on the hop farm in Beltring as soon as Hitler began his blizkrieg on 10 May 1940, we were to remain as anti-parachutist forces in our present position until the next October.

This suited me well. I had not taken kindly to Army life - the red tape, the inspections and other routine procedures irked my independence. However, when I was found the proper niche in the QVRs' as Quarter Master's Clerk-cum-Storeman, (with at Kennington, the added duty of Canteen Manager), I felt I was of some use and was quite willing to work long hours at congenial work, instead of resenting arms drill and bayonet practice.

So it was a rude shock when on the evening of 21st. May an air-raid warning disturbed our peace, the first I'd heard since the fateful 3rd. September 1939. This, sent us parading with steel hat, gas mask and rifle, (the pitiful precautions of 1940) in to the farmyard. An even ruder shock came when we were then told, when the 'All Clear' promised a return to bed, that we had five hours to get ready to go overseas.

I don't think I was scared. I was more annoyed than anything else that my plans should be disturbed. All my arrangements for my next leave were made - why should the British Army or the German High Command, or who ever was responsible, disturb them?

There was no time for more than these thoughts. Company Sergeant Major 'Tex' Austin who occupied part of the Company Office was distributing to each man a hundred rounds of live ammunition in a bandolier and thirty for the pouches. I collected mine in an interval from dashing upstairs and down between our office and a Company lorry and trying to get all the essential paraphenalia and stores attached to a Quartermaster's office loaded up, at the same time taking nothing unimportant. But I found room for the remains of that day's canteen stock of cakes which later I sold on a farm somewhere near Calais - the proceeds eventually going to the authorities of Stalag XXA - but I am going too fast.

When I had time to get ready myself, I found most of the Company already under way. I forget whether I travelled by motor-cycle or lorry to Ashford station - the latter I believe - but what a shock awaited the QVRs' there.

The QVRs' were a motor-cycle battalion which only received its full complement of motor-cycles and combinations, together with proper Army trucks, almost at the end of our spell at Beltring. These had replaced the converted grocery wagons and laundry vans which had served hitherto. I, an imported KRR militiaman, abominated motor-cycles (though tolerated lorries), but to the QVR Territorials all vehicles were a pride and joy.[2] To them it was an almost crushing blow to learn that the vehicles were to remain in England. I saw that all our stores were loaded up and then went along to a compartment where, with Norris and some other Riflemen, I slept fitfully until the next day, Wednesday 22nd.May, dawned.

There was no doubt in our minds of our destination. We understood that Hitler was advancing steadily so we were quite prepared to find ourselves as re-inforcements for the B.E.F. (British Expeditionary Force). It was no surprise on that grey morning to arrive at Dover where I bought, for the first time in my life *The Times* the only newspaper available. An account of the disastrous battle confirmed that the German armies were well advanced, but from the map, we judged them several hundred miles from our destination which we correctly surmised to be Calais.

At Dover I was shepherded with other Riflemen to a special hall whre I was issued with a cup of tea and some chocolate. The latter I had as breakfast, but it transpired later it was intended as 'haversack' rations. A long period of waiting followed. I with many others moved from point to point, (unless turned away by a fussy 'red-cap'), saw the boats waiting in the dock, contacted pals in B. and D. Companies and wrote a hasty note to my parents on the back of an envelope.[3]

This, my farewell, was received a few days later with heartache.

Eventually we were on board, and like others went below for a wash and shave. When I reappeared, I had no time for melancholia over a last glimpse of the white cliffs of Dover, as I was made busy changing the special gas-proof clothing issued to motor-cyclists for infantry gas capes. As far as I remember, we had docked before I had finished. I found myself gazing for the first time at a foreign country, and the shape of the half-ruined buildings of Calais station.

After C.Company stores were unloaded, Colour Sergeant Granger and I took charge of them. I was left guarding the pile of miscellaneous accessories while my chief went off to seek instructions from the Company commander. The three Company cooks, L/Cpl. Trend, Rifleman Jackson and Rifleman Williams, were found who had the containers of ham and peas, but the rest of the Company, in fact most of the Battalion, had vanished from my ken.

It was about this time I received my first shock. With one platform of Calais station practically in the sole occupation of the cooks and myself, it was peaceful in the warm sun, as the air raid warnings and 'All-clears' which had been sounding almost continuously since our arrival, had ceased. At the first warning, we had taken cover, but later the sirens sounded with such frequency that we had tended to ignore them.

The shock came when a party of stretcher-bearers disembarked from a train arriving at the station out of the blue with some horribly wounded men. These were not from our regiment, but I had not expected fresh blood to flow in front of me so quickly. Remember I had just left pre-Dunkirk, laissez-faire Britain which had been free from invasion since 1066.

We asked the wounded what the fighting was like. The reply was not encouraging. "B...... awful. They just let you carry on and you think everythings O.K.; then when you've gone too far to get back, they let you have it. It's just murder. I'm glad I'm out of it." This couldn't be true, could it? Or, if it was, it couldn't happen to us. In any case, the fighting must be miles away, we had a breathing space. These were my thoughts.

The next move was to transfer all our stores off the platform to the yard at the side. There, we saw a platoon of B.Company which however soon moved off. C/Sgt. Granger secured a lorry from somewhere and set off with two of the cooks to find C.Company headquarters. To my surprise I found it was now about five o'clock. Stranded in a foreign land with a collection of camouflage nets, office equipment and a large amount of Army paraphernalia with one cook for company, I felt very lonely. A small detachment of Royal Artillery arrived and offered to let us join them, but I was not inclined to leave the stores unattended. Night began to fall.

Eventually, about nine o'clock I was delighted to see C/Sgt. Granger arrive with a lorry. The cooks and Major Brown were alone at Company headquarters and we were to join them. Quickly loading the stores, Williams and I climbed aboard and the lorry bumped along winding lanes on a route which I have never been able to re-trace.

We passed through a farm gate and came to rest by a Dutch barn. The cooks were preparing a meal, so I unloaded the stores, hoping for a meal and sleep. Whilst this was happening the rest of the Company H.Q. arrived, very footsore, having marched from the station a considerable distance away; something I had not realised in the lorry.

As the least fatigued person, I was immediately put on guard at the end of the lane by the gate whilst my comrades-in-arms rested and had their supper. Only Company H.Q. had come to the farm, the remaining platoons being distributed at various strategic points. Eventually I was relieved - but only for my supper. A piece of bread, some ham and peas were hastily scooped into my mess tin, and just as quickly consumed.

Then I was given my next job. C/Sgt. Granger was to go round to the other platoons to give them their meals. Major Brown was accompanying him and I was to go as interpreter if any French were needed. I doubted whether the French which had taken me through 'matric' five years previously would stand the test.

The only foreigner we encountered on the road was a Belgian motor-cyclist who was very vague about where he had come from, or indeed where he was going. I have often wondered since if he were a 'fifth columnist'.[4] At one point I was sent into a shop to seek directions and there obtained some chocolate from a terrified French woman.

I found it an exciting and exhilarating experience driving round the French lanes, stopping at cross-roads to unload the food containers to shadowy figures who proved to be friends from Platoons 8 and 9. Platoon 10 was more difficult to find, but in the end these too were contacted.

My clearest memory of that Wednesday night was of the song of the nightingales. A town dweller, I had never heard that sweetest of all bird songs except over the wireless, until that night in Calais. The beauty of that song was a memory which often cheered me in the dark hours to come. There must be hope for a world now bent on destruction, if nightingales could sing.

We returned to the C.Company H.Q. and I was at last allowed to crawl on to the straw to sleep, but with equipment and rifle beside me and boots on my feet.

The next day dawned too quickly for me. After a sketchy breakfast - tinned bacon and bread I believe-I arranged the stores which had been left unsorted. I was called away to parade with the remainder of the platoon for rifle inspection, and realised with sorrow that my exemption from such parades was at an end.

The events of Thursday and Friday are now rather mixed in my memory. At first we were all busily engaged in digging trenches, but since L/Cpl. Kempner thought he could do better on his own, I returned to my stores. Planes coming over caused some excitement to the anti-aircraft defence - a single Bren gun in a pit installed by Kempner.

He spotted some suspicious individuals on the horizon and turned the Bren on them. Later it was seen by Major Hamilton through binoculars that a woman was being carried away by civilians. I was momentarily horrified by this incident but consoled myself with the thought they might have been 'fifth columnists'.

During the morning we were allowed to go to a school at the end of the lane leading to the farm which was occupied by a small detachment of French troops, (thought to be Ack Ack, i.e.an Anti-aircraft emplacement). Here we were to wash. I heard later that Major Brown had made an agreement with the French that neither party would evacuate their position without informing the other.

In the morning we were visited by the Regimental Sergeant Major who issued 'Field Postcards' to us which stated that we were alive and well. At that time I thought that this provision of postcards so soon after our arrival was a triumph of organisation. In fact the cards never left France.

After a frugal dinner I was ordered on guard duty for an hour, most of which I spent at the farm gate watching the ducks and hens. When I came off guard, I found orders had been given to evacuate, and that the French had departed without informing us. This was the reason for our own move.

We were told to leave everything except our equipment and rifles and to hurry over fields led by our officers. We struggled through wire fences and eventually arrived at a main road along which French vehicles were moving at high speed. After several attempts Major Brown managed to stop one vehicle to enquire what had happened to cause the panic and where the convoy was bound. No very coherent reply was received in English or French.

A British staff car now appeared and an officer ordered us back to our former position at the farm. So we all re-traced our steps. We passed numerous shell holes which we had not noticed on our outward journey so assumed the farm had been shelled in our absence, though the buildings had been miraculously spared.

We spent the night in the straw of the Dutch barn, and I had probably a better sleep than before or later. On Friday morning the Battalion Padre, who I had only earlier seen at Church parades at East Peckham church, appeared. All available men, of which I was one, paraded for a service in the orchard close to the farm. It was very much based on the theme of "Onward Christian Soldiers", which we sang lustily, and gave me the impression of giving us the last rites before our imminent deaths.

The feeling was re-inforced when ten or more of us were formed into a platoon, climbed into a small civilian van which had presumably been commandeered. We were taken to a field behind a hedge commanding a view of a narrow road below. We were told that three German tanks were expected and if we successfully put them out of action our mission would be complete.

Our only weapons were our rifles and one Bren gun, which I had never fired, so I doubted whether our fire power would be able to stop one tank, let alone three! It proved to be a false alarm, the tanks did not come, and we were thankful to return to the van and the farm.

On Friday afternoon, Major Brown decided to take all the men of Company Headquarters on a reconnaissance, leaving L/Cpl. Norris in charge at the farm. He called for a Rifleman to stay with Norris to resist any Germans whilst the main party was away.

I volunteered, not as an act of bravery but because I was convinced we had no chance of coming through alive and thought I might as well await death in reasonable comfort. I could see no sense in careering over fields again with no apparent objective. If the Germans did come, it seemed to me most unlikely that we two with our rifles would have any chance, of putting up any effective resistence. I was prepared to go through the motions which was not commendable but I was just past caring. Nevertheless I was glad when the others wearily returned after some hours having seen no Germans.

At some point on Thursday or Friday we heard a rumour that we were to be re-placed by Canadians and were to return to England. Later I heard that there had been the intention to send over Canadians but not to re-place us. I have heard that the only reason we were sent at all, being untried material, was that we were unlucky enough to be the nearest infantry to Dover.

Across the fields to the left of the farm we could see thick black smoke rising from what we feared were burning oil tanks in Boulogne. Whether this was so we did not know, but the smoke was certainly at Boulogne, defended as I later heard by the Guards, some of whom we met in captivity. After the War I found out that the farm and all the positions held by C.Company during, Wednesday, Thursday and Friday, were to the east of Calais, but of this I had no idea at the time.

As night fell, we were paraded and told that we were to support the 60th. Rifles in a counter-attack. We were to leave our packs and haversacks at the farm and take only essential equipment and weapons. We marched off in single file and so continued for a while but with long haltsfrom time to time. We finished up in the dock area of Calais, though I have read since that it was not a counter-attack but a withdrawal from the outer perimeter through the lines held by the 60th. Rifles.

I think day had already dawned by the time we stopped marching, but very soon vehicles appeared with our kit aboard, so we were able to wash and shave. Soon after, we had our first taste of action as the German Air Force took a hand. It sent over waves of Stukas which dived at us. The noise of their engines and the bullets was devastating and we all dived for cover. I fell under a lorry and lay there in panic until the aircraft had gone. It was probably a senseless place to but the fact of having something between me and the sky was a comfort. The strange thing is that I do not think any bombs were released nor anyone killed or wounded. We were given no orders to fire and any confidence we British may have had was certainly dissipated.

From this time on, our operations lost any cohesion there had been up to now. We were ordered to make our way as quickly as possible down an alley between two high warehouses and were warned that we were in danger from snipers. Halfway along the alley we met some British armoured vehicles coming towards us. They had been instructed to withdraw and allowed us to jump on their vehicles and were thus carried back to our starting point. There we were met by an irate officer who made us dismount and go back along the alley.

We rushed along, neither knowing or caring where we were going until we came to a square with a large church. We were directed to cross the square and were fired upon. It turned out that the bullets came from some KRRC men and not the Germans, some of my comrades being hit. We came to some railway sidings where Major Hamilton gave us orders to put on gas-masks as he believed there was some. This was another false alarm and we were very glad to remove the masks as they were very hot with the afternoon sun and our exertions.

Then we made our way to the railway sidings where we were put into position under goods wagons commanding a view of some water, probably the one marked 'Bassin' on a map of Calais.

I found myself now beside Riflemen I did not know, and assume they were from the Rifle Brigade since it seems they were primarily in charge of eastern Calais; the 60th. Rifles were responsible fot the west.

Surprisingly, it did not occur to me to talk to men on my right or left but merely lay in the dust under the wagon with my rifle at the ready. Feeling so fatalistic I willingly accompanied an unknown NCO (non-commissioned officer) who ordered me to go with him to draw rations for myself and my immediate companions. I do not know why he chose me, but supposed that as a Rifle Brigade corporal, he had more confidence in his own men who were 'Regulars', than he had of me to repel Germans, a member of a Territorial battalion with no fighting experience.

I discovered that there were warehouses at the rear of the complex of railway lines, the NCO leading me through a gap between two warehouses to a narrow alley. There he stopped because of a burst of fire from the right. After this stopped, we dashed across to the next gap between warehouses where we were protected until we came to the next alley under fire from the right. Once again we crossed during a lull.

Following the corporal to a doorway through which was a room with cans of bully beef and beer. I had to return alone and so was left to judge when to cross and avoid each hail of bullets. Doubtless, I handed over food and drink to the riflemen near me, and suppose I had some myself, but can not recall doing so.

I lay there as it became dark, straining my eyes to detect any signs of the enemy. At one stage I thought I saw movement and the sound of oars from the water, but could not be sure; there was no reaction from the men around me so I stayed silent until able to report it to an NCO who came along. He did not take it seriously, believing that I had dozed off and dreamt it. As I may well have done! At the time I was convinced, but now it seems illogical as surely some of us would have heard the Germans coming ashore.

So the night of Saturday passed peacefully. After it was light, orders were given to withdraw into the town. Of course there was no breakfast, and indeed I did not eat or drink that day.

We found the town in chaos under fire from artillery or mortars. Walls were falling and the roads strewn with bricks and wires. As I followed my companions through this devastation, I was surprised to meet Rifleman Johnson who had been in my training squad at Winchester, but then posted to the KRRC. We exchanged a few words then re-joined our respective contingents.

I and half a dozen other riflemen were sent into a building which was still standing and were installed in a large room on the upper floor with windows fronting the street. Once again, we were to await the arrival of a few German tanks on which we were to fire. The apartment was certainly a more comfortable place to await the enemy than the railway tracks. It was absolutely luxurious with a thick carpet and a white and gold furniture. There was a half full bottle of wine on a table, and a smell of scent and women, so it was concluded by some of the others that we were in a brothel. Having no experience of such places, I assumed this to be right.

As the conviction was growing by the minute that I expected to be killed at any time, I hoped we should have a short spell of comfort. But this was not to be. Very soon we were ordered from our vantage point, down the stairs, out of the door and then down into a cellar. High up on one side were windows from which we were once again ordered to fire on any German tanks.

CAPTURE

On Sunday, 26th. May 1940, I was in the cellar of a house in Calais with a handful of fellow riflemen. I counted myself lucky to be alive after four days of horror since we had landed at the port, days in which I had been machine gunned by Stukas, shot at by snipers on many occasions, and latterly bombarded by mortars and artillery. I did not count very highly my chances of survival when a British officer unknown to me shouted to us to throw away the bolts of our rifles and come up to surrender. We emerged to find the streets a sea of green uniformed Germans with tanks, motorcycles and many types of four-wheeled vehicles.

To become a prisoner-of-war is a chastening experience. I had a mixed feeling of humiliation and guilt as an Englishman capitulating, apprehension for our treatment and relief at no longer having to attempt to kill others, or of being in imminent danger of being killed myself, and a great weariness. At that time I did not feel hungry although I had had little to eat in Calais or in fact since we had left the farm in Kent. Food however was to become a major pre-occupation.

Apart from relieving us of our equipment, in general the Germans did not take our personal possessions. We had to stand with our hands on our heads whilst the search was carried out which gave me the first chance of a close look at the enemy. Two things struck me. Firstly, that the German helmet fitted closely over the top and back of the head, so providing greater protection than our own 'tin hats'. Secondly, that their belts were kept in place by a silver coloured buckle bearing the words "Gott mit uns"; "God with us" was thus an equivalent of our hymn "Onward Christian Soldiers".

However, the search complete, there was no time for philosophy. We were formed up in to fives and counted, the first of hundreds of such counts, at which the Germans were by no means very good. Then with the word "Los" which was to become all too familiar with us, (a colloquial expression meaning "Get going") we set off over the roads of France.

Although quite shattered by the catastrophe that had befallen, we all seemed to seek the companionship of men known to us. The columns of five became something of a shambles, so it was possible to change one's position in response to shouts of "QVRs here". The men however I found myself with were only casual aquaintances since they were not militiamen with whom I had been transferred.

As we walked along, I did suggest that as it became dark, it would be possible to leave the columns in the spaces between the guards who walked at either side at intervals, perhaps on the excuse of a call of nature. None responded to this suggestion and I did not have the nerve to try it alone; in retrospect I would perhaps have had more chance on my own. I have condemned myself for my lack of courage at that time.

We were still proceeding (not marching) when darkness fell and were ultimately allowed to stop and lie down at the side of the road. I must have fallen asleep immediately for the next thing I remember were shouts of "Aufstehen", ("Stand up"). It was then that I discovered I had been lying on a pile of stones intended for road mending, but was totally unaware of it.

On the second day we were marched through villages where the people put out buckets of water with cups to enable us to drink. Sometimes the Germans allowed us to do so but eventually a less civilised guard would kick over the buckets.

It seems that we were marched in a generally southern direction from Calais as we saw signs pointing to Montreuil. The column was stopped and we were turned into a large field through which a stream ran. There was some concern among us because it was suggested that this was an ideal spot for the Germans to machine gun us, and wiping us out well away from buildings and onlookers. In fact we were given a kind of soup for which we had to queue with whatever container we had. The only thing I had was my tin hat, so I cut out the leather inside and put my finger over the knob at the top. I suppose, whilst I did not have a mess tin, I must have retrieved my eating utensils, as I am sure I spooned up the soup, and certainly the Germans supplied nothing.

I was able to wash out my tin hat making use of the stream and washed myself. Some washed their clothes but I did not do so although it was sunny and we did not know how long we would be there.

On one of the first two days of the march, I wrote a note to my parents on a card I found in my pocket. Much depressed and believing I would never see them again, I thanked them for all their kindness and said I must now put my trust in God's mercy. I was able to hand it to a French civilian, but it did not reach home until after I was officially registered as a prisoner by the Germans - and this was some weeks and many miles away.

My father carefully kept all the cards and letters they received, and I still have them except for that first postcard, although my mother later referred to it as that "terrible card" and perhaps it was destroyed as being an emotional outbreak in a time of great stress. I now think its destruction was a pity as one's fears of imminent death or indefinite confinement concentrate the mind wonderfully and express one's most sincere thoughts.

We were marched off again on the third day and finished up in another field where we were each given a packet of 'knackerbrot', (not unlike 'Ryvita'). It was the first solid food we had received since capture so we ate it quickly in spite of no water to wash it down.

It rained that night but I was fortunate to find a place under a hedge which kept me comparitively dry. I woke early being cold, damp and miserable and wandered around, but was soon cheered by suddenly meeting Ted Lyme who had become quite a friend at

Beltring. I think he was equally enthusiastic at this meeting and we resolved forthwith to share and share alike in future. Our comradeship over the next nine months or so was a God-send.

It was now Wednesday, 29th. May, and for the next week we were marched along poplar-lined French roads for the whole day finding places to stop at night. Fortunately it did not rain again as far as I can re-call. Sometimes we were able to obtain drinks of water or even food from the French in the villages. On one occasion I was able to rush into a village shop and buy a packet of butter, and on another a bottle of Vichy water, before being chased out by the guards.

From time to time we did receive some food from the Germans such as soup, bread or biscuits, but always it involved standing in a long queue. We found it essential to guard our small stock of provisions, especially when put in the same field or building as the French or Belgians. It was much easier being in a partnership of two, each trusting the other, so that one stayed with our possessions whilst the other searched for anything useful. On one of his forays, Ted found a large piece of grey canvas which had belonged to some Frenchmen. The British had been captured with the minimum of possesions because of the action in which they had been involved, whilst the French were in much better shape being equipped with blankets, groundsheets and mess-tins as if they had prepared themselves for captivity. It would have been quite impossible to have participated in a running battle and have retained all this equipment. Thus neither Ted nor I had any scruples about taking this canvas.

It was certainly the first time I had ever been involved in theft - though we referred to it as having been 'acquired'. This was the foundation of a 'prisoner-of-war' mentality which has remained with me until now and will remain until my dying day. It is something that all prisoners-of-war share. I will say that I am neither proud nor sorry of having developed this attitude because I think it was almost inevitable in the circumstances. That piece of canvas became one of our most prized possessions.

Although in the early stages of the march we were put into open fields from which we might have escaped if we had been able to dodge patrols and not been too exhausted, the field in which we acquired the blanket cum groundsheet was a wired-in compound and patrolled.

Some prisoners tried to bargain with the guards for food in exchange for watches and rings. There may have been some advantageous deals but some prisoners lost valuables without any recompense. Of course there was no redress.

When I was captured I was determined not to reveal my three years of German at school. The most we had done was learn German songs. I felt at this time that I might overhear the guards talking and understand enough to help me to escape.This was a fallacy and I now realise that if I had revealed my knowledge I might have been given interpreter status and some favours in food.

In the early days of the march, the roads were quite congested with many French civilians fleeing with their possesions on carts, barrows and bicycles which they pushed to the side to let us pass. The columns of prisoners had to give way when necessary to military vehicles passing in both directions. We could not but be overawed by their size, power and quality. The German motor-cycle combinations looked to me to be in a far superior class to the Nortons on which I trained on Wiltshire and Kent roads.

At Hesdin we spent the night in the football stadium althought the terraces were not too comfortable. The night after I bought the Vichy water I felt very sick, probably as a result of drinking fizzy liquid after biscuits piled with butter. Most of us had blisters as a result of marching and stumbling over cobbled roads, but there was no relief until we stopped on Wednesday, 5th. June.

Most of the people on the march had been captured in or around Calais, and as we had been at Winchester, Bushfield Camp and Chiseldon with the KRRC, and at Beltring and Ashford with the QVR, we knew many people slightly, though few intimately. We had many different companions and exchanged our experiences, and it was sad to hear of friends who had been killed. I was distressed to hear of Johnson's death as we had shared a room in my first weeks at Winchester and with whom we used to visit an old lady for afternoon tea.

On Thursday 6th. June we were at last given the chance of reporting sick. Ted and I took the opportunity; the examination was cursory and we

P.O.W.Camp

Stalag XXI D

Photographs by kind permission of the Imperial War Museum

Stalag VIII B.

Sports Day at Camp Willenberg

were taken a short distance to a railway where we were told to board a platform truck, that is a platform on a bogey but with no sides. On adjoining similar vehicles were many French and Belgian prisoners loaded with luggage. It was inconceivable that all these people were classified as sick. Possibly the Germans thought they had marched their prisoners far enough from the combat zone. Later, I heard that the British we had left behind were only marched one or two days more and then transported as we were.

Ted and I were happy to rest in comparitive comfort as we were transported eastwards for nearly a day. The train stopped at frequent intervals and once we, the British were made to dismount. Then a German officer came up to address the Belgians and French in French, but not being his native language he spoke slowly and I was therefore able to understand the gist of his tirade. He told his audience that the blame lay with the British who had deserted their allies and left them in the lurch. Although we received some black looks, we suffered nothing more, possibly they had not yet heard of the Dunkirk evacuation. In due

course we were allowed to return to the platform truck and the journey continued.

We travelled through the night and dozed off at intervals, despite the bed being very hard. We were awake when we passed through Luxemburg which was full of light and seemed like a fairy tale city which I confirmed nearly forty years later. Early on the Friday we arrived at Trier of which I had never heard. When I re-visited it many years later I found it had been the Roman capital of the region because of its strategic position on the River Mosel and possesses a wealth of ancient buildings from Roman times to the 16th. and 17th. centuries.

Our stay at Trier was short. From the station we marched uphill on a cobbled road and was somewhat ashamed to see some of the British scrambling in the gutter for cigarette ends; but then I was not a smoker. We were taken to a large field where there were many POWs of different nationalities. It pleased us to be able to join the other British as we had felt like pariahs among the French and Belgians.

We were given bowls of soup consisting of greasy

water with lumps of fat pork floating in it. In our hunger we consumed this greedily but it certainly made me ill later. We were also given a bread ration for which we queued. It was as well that there were two of us able to claim a fair share as the fifth person was left with a very small portion. Some managed to re-join the queue and so obtain a second helping, in consequence a few went without, since the Germans had made a head-count, divided by five and thus produced the requisite number of portions.

Before nightfall we were formed into fives again and marched to the station where we were crammed into cattle trucks at a ratio of eighty men per wagon. Ted and I found a place in a corner which provided a rough seat; there was just room for each man to stand or sit.

I began to feel ill, probably due to a combination of fat pork and the exhaustion of the last sixteen days aince Calais. The only place to lie down was under the seat, and even there was in danger of being accidentally kicked and used the bag containing my few possessions and bread ration as a pillow.

I dozed fitfully during the night and all the next day and part of the one after that. I believe the doors of the wagon were opened once for toilet purposes but men had to perform from it and were not allowed down. I heard from other men on my first working party that the train stopped at Berlin and German Red Cross nurses provided coffee, but I have no recollection of this. I was semi-conscious throughout the journey, but the enforced rest did me good and allowed me to clamber out of the wagon with Ted. We heard what were to become the German shouts of "Aufstehen" and "Rous" [Get up. Out] which were to become only too familiar.

I found that we were at a station with the name of Thorn [pronounced Torn.], the former Polish town of Torun on the River Vistula in the Polish corridor devised at the Treaty of Versailles to allow Poland access to the Baltic Sea. Next to the station were imposing iron gates through which we were marched to find ourselves inside a fort which we came to know as Fort 17.

THE LONG MARCH TO FREEDOM

Until the end of 1944, life at Zempelburg, outside Thorn, continued to follow the pattern of 1943, both with in and around the factory at a level with which we as long-term prisoners could cope, leaving us reasonable time for our cooking and entertainment. We had not received our Christmas Red Cross parcels, but we had had ordinary parcels so did not go hungry. I wrote home on 7th. January 1945 to tell my parents that the Christmas parcels had made a belated appearance and also that I had received from them a personal parcel of two hundred cigarettes. We had resumed work on 27th. December 1944, but there had seemed less enthusiasm among our German foremen to press on with the work for the Reich than formerly; from the Polish workmen we heard constantly of the Russians' advance.

On 26th. January, one of my fellow prisoners, Pedlar Palmer, who cleaned a bicycle belonging to one of the Germans, brought the rumour that the whole camp would be moving. We had stopped without any reason being given, and during the day and throughout the following night, small parties of British prisoners were brought in from outlying farms and had to make themselves comfortable on the floor of various barrack rooms. They had brought with them sheep and pigs, as well as the carcases of slaughtered animals on carts, the meat being well frozen in the sub-zero conditions.

The following morning, 27th January, we were told we were to move immediately, taking with us everything we could carry whether food, clothing or blankets. We were issued with our best uniforms, boots and greatcoats normally kept in store and only worn for a special occasion, such as a visit to the dentist or hospital, or for the occasional trip a few of us made by train to visit the Headquarters Camp at Thorn.[Now Torun].

I augmented these nearly new outer garments with two sets of underclothing, two pullovers, a scarf and a balaclava helmet. I had sewn a pair of braces to my kitbag for ease of carrying, so I crammed this with my two blankets and such socks and underclothing as I could push in. I had also a couple of haversacks for washing and toilet kit, a Bible and whatever food I could carry from our Red Cross stocks although some bulky packets and heavy tins had to be left behind. We had too our bread ration for five days, namely one large rye bread loaf.

We paraded and were counted outside the camp and I suppose the Germans satisfied themselves that we were all there, but in their anxiety to leave and the confusion of the additional farm workers several men were able to absent themselves from the roll-call. They had girl friends among the Polish workers and planned to hide in the barracks until we had left, then join them in the village. I learned after my return that this occurred in other work parties in Poland but it appears that most of them were picked up by the Russians with whom they had an unpleasant time. Efforts were made to force them to fight with the Russians which they resisted and this did not endear them to their allies. They were transported eastwards and re-patriated to Britain from Odessa, arriving home well after VE Day.

My own attitude, and I think it was shared by the majority, and I think it was shared by the majority, was that I would rather stay in the hands of thenGermans with whom I had been able to survive without too much discomfort for four and a half years, than risk being at the mercy of the Russians. I had strong anti-Communist feelings in my adolescent years and great antipathy to the Hitler-Stalin pact which led to the invasion of Poland.

Moreover, those few Russian prisoners I had seen appeared to be uncouth, degraded beings whom we ostracised. We did not fully appreciate that we would perhaps have been no better, if we had not had our Red Cross parcels.

It was something of a blow to leave the compartive cosiness of our life at Zempelburg; our work was not too unpleasant or onerous, our quarters reasonably comfortable, food was sufficient with the Red Cross parcels and our leisure time occupied with cooking, reading, cards, theatrical productions etc.. However, I believe that no-one regretted it, as we were aware from the German newspapers and factory gossip that the Russians were advancing in our direction. Hopefully we would go westwards towards our own forces.

Nevertheless, it was a daunting prospect to be marched off in the snow at a temperature of 35 degrees of frost Fahrenheit (-19.5 degrees C) with only those possessions we could carry. It was some comfort to know that our German guards were in the same position and feared the Russians more than we did. I heard later that, as we left the camp at one end of Zempleburg, the Russians marched in at the other end. Two who had hidden in the camp were picked up by the Russians who set fire to the buildings. Two others went into the town but I do not know what happened to them; as they were experienced regulars they may well have survived.

We had several farm wagons from the outlying farms, which the Germans had commandeered. On one of these live pigs and sheep were to serve as food in the next few days. The Germans dumped their belongings on the other wagons. In the thick snow, there was no question of marching or keeping in any formation. As we stumbled along we heard bursts of firing not far away, whereupon the guards urged us on by pointing tommy guns at us. I had the feeling, although we were not tired and demoralised as on the 1940 march, a foolish resistance or argument could have provoked a shot. Not all the guards were trigger-happy though.

I heard that the Germans were under orders to proceed for five days to Neu-Stettin. [In Polish Szczecinek]. Through out this account, I shall refer to the German names of places which I was able to note down from the signs which they had erected at the boundary of each settlement. [They were in black letters on a yellow ground]. In England the threat of invasion had caused the removal of signposts in 1940, although I doubt whether this would have delayed an advancing German army. Probably the Russians had advanced more quickly than expected and so the Germans did not have time.

We struggled on through the snow and some, both British and Germans, threw away part of their possessions to lighten their loads. Jim Thomas (Thomo) who had been my mucker [that is trusted companion] since 1941, sharing kit and food parcels, fell over and was allowed to ride on a wagon for a time. Then a more needy casualty replaced him, but Thomo managed to get the job of driving the horses on a wagon. As a result he was given a hot drink at Linde, the place we were scheduled to spend the first night. The Russians however were deemed to be too near so we had to continue.

By evading the guards I was able to put my kitbag on to the wagon until we eventually arrived at a barn in Dubrin. I think we had some hot stew, the cooking of which had been started at Linde; then we found places to lie in the straw fully clothed with our boots on because the roof had many gaps in it, so snow came in and melted on us.

I heard that the ration of German sausage intended for us had been commandeered by the guards. When I awoke I found that my feet were more or less frozen to my boots, but that morning we were on our way again without even a hot drink. Thomo was driving the wagon again, but once more I had to carry my kitbag.

We were now crossing an open stretch of country with a howling wind blowing snow into our faces, so we could only edge forward with the greatest difficulty. Someone noticed my nose was frostbitten and insisted I rub it with snow, which certainly saved it.

There was no road to follow but the guards seemed to have had some idea because, after what seemed hours of struggling, we arrived at the village of Stretzin where the buildings gave us some shelter from wind and snow. We crowded into doorways where some of the civilians gave us coffee. The guards realising we could not travel further that day found us billets in a barn of a saw - mill which was dry. A meal was prepared of mutton broth and potatoes and we ate this gratefully.

There were many cases of frostbite and when I took off my boots and socks to dry them, as we had found a stove, I noticed that my big toes were affected. Thomo, who had appointed himself assistant to the camp Medical Orderly, decided they must be rubbed with snow.

By the evening we had made ourselves comfortable, but at about 9 p.m. we were made to move a short distance to a hay loft which was both dry and warm. So on our second night we had a good, comfortable sleep. Someone had acquired an oil lamp which was very useful, but quite a fire hazard.

Next morning, I was one of the few who climbed down the ladder for a wash in the icy water from a tap in the yard. My frostbitten feet were in a bad way, so I was allowed to ride on a wagon except when we came to hills. I had Thomo's kit on the wagon with me

as he had lost his job as a driver. Many people tried to put their kit on the cart and I helped them when I could, but of course this slowed our progress. On this third day we were passed by a party from Marienwerder who had been eight days on the road, and I commented in my diary, "What will it be like if we have to do 8 days?" Little did I know how many days it would be!

We passed a party of American prisoners, then stopped for the night in a barn twelve kilometres from Hammerstein. I had travelled all day on the wagon with two dead pigs and a dead calf under me, and now the volunteer butchers cut them up and a meal of meat, potatoes and peas was to be prepared. We heard it would not be ready until the morning, so after I had had my feet treated we found snug billets and turned in at six in the evening.

At 10 p.m. we were rudely awakened by the guards shouting, "In zehn Minuten, sind alles raus. Los da!" ["Everybody out in ten minutes. Hurry up!"]. Some people tried to grab some of the food being cooked, but I made for the sick wagon. The Germans were determined that progress was not to be delayed by an overloaded wagon, so I was only allowed to put my kit on it.

We had a nightmare journey all through the night in deep snow. People were continually falling back and then being chased to catch up. When I was pushed by a guard, I feigned collapse (although it was really my feet bothering me) and I was put on the wagon where it was terribly cold but better than stumbling through the snow.

We reached the outskirts of Hammerstein and joined a party from Rasmin. Our sick were moved on to their wagon because the rubber tyres of ours were in bad shape. Hammerstein had evidently been a camp for American prisoners. We travelled a good distance into the main camp. After a lengthy delay billets in huts were found for us at 6.30 a.m. We were told that we would stay there all day.

It was 30th. January, and a party of POWs from Graudenz were just leaving as we arrived. They had received four Red Cross parcels each, and as they could not carry 40 lbs. each they gave us some of the heavier items, such as tins of milk and fish to keep us going. We were not at all unhappy to be back in a camp again even for a short time, because now we had shelter, toilets and washing facilities. It appeared that a number of parties used Hammerstein as a transit camp. The Germans had obviously decided that this was an easy way to provide food for their prisoners and prevent it falling into advancing Russian hands.

One worry we had was that we would be left resting in the hut whilst the distribution of parcels to our party was taking place, so either Thomo or myself left the hut to forage around and find out our turn. In all the years as a POW there was conflicting information from our own NCOs and the guards, so it was absolutely essential that only one of us left the hut at any time leaving the other to watch over our possessions, as there were also Russian POWs in the camp.

I had seen very few of them during my captivity, and those I had seen had been housed in compounds well away from the British, or else had been in transit in cattle trucks. As there were only a few of them visiting our hut, I guessed they had broken out of their own barbed wire section in search of food. As we had been given more than we could use that day and were expecting to receive our own parcels, we were willing to give them some of our tins. However I found whilst one would be taking a tin from me and thanking me profusely, two more were behind me trying to help themselves. Fortunately as there were more British than Russians and we were in better condition, we were able to clear them out of our huts, but it was a nasty reminder of 1940 when all but one's closest friends were potential threats.

Eventually the word spread that we were to queue for our parcels at a certain time, and we duly received one parcel each. I believe that some went to the back of the queue after receiving their parcels and so obtained a second one as the Germans had less interest in accurate counting. However, Thomo and I took the view that an extra 10 lbs of food each was more than enough to add to our loads. Some men were clever enough to construct make-shift sleds from the wooden parcel boxes and used them whilst the snow lasted.

Having had rest and food at Hammerstein, we marched away happily along roads badly blocked by German refugees with their possessions on wagons, reminding us of the French in 1940.

When we were unable to proceed further, we found shelter at the bottom of the hill in a doorway where some people obtained cups of coffee, two of my friends sharing theirs with me. Thomo arrived with the wagon and I told him that there was coffee at the house, so he was able to beg some for himself and his sick passengers. Now we had to climb a terrific snow-clad slope where the road could not be seen. At the top our wagons became mixed up with the refugees and an Army convoy. Crossing a railway we reached the village of Kleinkudde. It was full of refugees, but we were able to bed down in the loft of a barn, with the refugees and their horses in the rest of the building. We talked to them for a while and realised they were in the same situation as us, needing food, drink and shelter.

The next day, January 31st., we pushed on to reach Neu Stettin which we had been told was our original destination. We passed through road blocks to enter the town. It was quite the biggest and best German town we had seen throughout our years as prisoners. It had big shops, with little or nothing in the windows and a theatre marked "Geschlossen" [Closed].

We saw, with considerable resentment, German soldiers unloading Red Cross parcels into shops for German consumption. This nevertheless was the only occasion I know or have heard of this happening, and believethat it was only now, desperate for food the Germans breached the Geneva Convention.

We went right through the town to a small village four km. beyond where we were billeted in a granary. Almost as soon as I had secured a good place to sleep, we were ordered to move on and returned towards Neu Stettin passing a stream of refugee carts. This time we skirted the town passing a magnificent tall mansion fronting peaceful parkland. Even at this time I thought how lovely it must have been in summer, regretting how much it would suffer in the Russian offensive.

We saw more road blocks on the other side of the town where we had entered it. Obviously, we had been taken along the wrong road. By now it was dark and very cold. A column of Serbian officers we had passed earlier when leaving Hammerstein told us in German that the Russians were blocking this road which would lead to Tempelburg. The Serbs passed on, followed by a column of French with sledges loaded with Red Cross parcels. It seemed to us that from 1940 onwards captured French soldiers always provided themselves with a greater degree of comfort than any other nationality.

Unfortunately, the diary I had kept during the last days of January came to an end. After fifty years, I am surprised that I had had the energy after a day's march to write notes about it. Hereafter I have only a list of places through which we passed to guide me, and even then there are gaps. From this list I see that after our manoeuvres round Neu Stettin, we spent the night at Hutton and the next at Baldon. The next two are blank., then we went on for four days and had our first rest day since Hammerstein. Obviously by now we had put a sufficient distance between us and the advancing Russians. We needed a rest as did the guards, most of whom had walked with us from Zempelburg. On 5th. February we reached Falkenburg, the next day Henkebruks via Dramburg, the next Rubnow via Wengarin, and on February 8th. Kratzig. The next three days are blank.

During the first ten days of February, our difficulties with snow lessened. The roads became clearer so those with home-made sleds had to abandon them. We still had to compete with streams of fleeing refugees, both for road space and accommodation. Sometimes we had a billet where they were in a barn whilst we had the loft above, and then we were able to barter with them who would take soap or cigarettes for bread and vegetables.

On the whole, the guards were now less vigilant at night, so we were able to move around the villages. This was not always the case and I remember once the British Sergeant-Major in nominal charge of us was beaten up by the Germans. From about 1942 non-commissioned officers (corporals and above) were no longer forced to work. Some however chose to do so as a way of passing the time and this man had obviously found an acceptable way of life on one of the farms near Zempelburg. There we had had one Sergeant who was the senior soldier and he received instructions from the Germans, so he did no physical work.

Most of our nights were spent in barns or lofts which were reasonably warm. The main snag was that we had only one or two paraffin lamps, so when men needed to get up in the night they had some difficulty reaching the exit. One of my friends, Bill

Forster, (always known as Beattie because of his fiancée's name tattooed on his forearm) fell through the loft opening. He broke some bones, so when we moved off in the morning he was left at the farm, ostensibly for transfer to a hospital, but I feared for his fate.

We had now reached the border between the old East Germany and Poland at the mouth of the River Oder. We were directed to pass through the islands connected to the mainland by bridges. We were told that it was a highly a highly sensitive military area and that anyone leaving the column or our billet would be shot. On 12th. February we stopped at Wollin on the island of that name, next at Swinemünde where we slept in a concert hall, and then on February 14th. to Usedom, and then off the island to Zarchfern. We did not know why these island were so important to the Germans, but realise now that it was there that the flying bombs and rockets were being tested. We were very glad to leave the islands and so the strict German discipline relaxed.

We were in Germany proper and were told that our destination was now the Lüneberger Heide.[5] We did not know where that was, nor did it help much that it was believed to be near Hanover which I vaguely believed to be in central Germany and a long way from the Oder.

How much the German authorities controlled our movements I do not know, we were just one of many parties of POWs moving away from the Russian advance. I suspect that many a German adjutant had a difficult time ensuring no two parties finished up at the same village for the night. It did happen though sometimes; I can remember spending one night in a brick-making factory where several parties of British were billeted. The parties were mixed up and I found myself beside a chap who told me that before joining the Army he had been a tramp, making his living by doing odd jobs on farms such as chopping wood. I suppose this was a better preparation for POW life than my years in an insurance office. We did not sleep well that night, although it was warm enough, because there were gaps in the floor through which we could see flames below.

Another night we spent in a football stadium where the guards were very relaxed and we had no difficulty in visiting nearby houses to do some bartering. Some of our woollens for which we had no longer any use served as currency for food. One of our stops was close to a large tenement occupied by refugees of all ages and nationalities. It was like a mediæval market place with people singing in one room, cutting hair in another, playing a guitar in a third, cooking or sleeping or playing cards. We wandered round without interference, but all these people were as poor as we were and had no food to barter.

The Germans did provide us with food when they could buy it and most of the time we at least had bread and coffee. However, we would have been hungry if we had not foraged for ourselves.

After the islands we passed through Greifswald, Grimmen, Demmin, Malchin and Waren which brought us to 26th. February when we had a rest day. We tried to wash and dry our clothes and generally clean ourselves up. The Germans usually required some fatigue parties and there were plenty volunteers as a visit to a small town might provide an opportunity to barter for food, or just take it.

We continued via Plau, Lubz, Parchin and Neustadt-Glene up to 5th. March and then I have a gap in my list of places on the route until 19th. March. During this time we had quite long periods of rest when we were billeted in a farm building at the end of the village. We were to send a set of underclothes to be laundered by the village washerwomen, and to do odd jobs for the local people. I volunteered and was taken to a garden to chop wood. I was left there without any supervision, so I worked away on the POW principle of having something to show when challenged, but plenty left to do.

After a time a young German woman, certainly no older than myself, came and invited me into the house for coffee. She had two young children who were having their morning rest and a mother living with her. Her husband was in the Army on the Eastern front and she had not heard from him for some time. The guard re-appeared so I had to return to work, Later on I was again invited into the house and given a bowl of soup, this time the mother and the children were present and we had no conversation, probably I thought mother would not approve.

Next day Thomo took my place but he did not receive an invitation into the house although he had his refreshment. He contrived to leave me some wood to chop next day but on this occasion I was given my coffee in the kitchen and there was no sign of the family. As I was alone I foraged in the pantry but could find nothing edible except for a few crusts of bread. In the end I did see her again, she showing me proudly a shelf of books in English. I was interested in these and she kindly lent me one. This was a rare treat as food for our minds could not be carried at the expense of food for our stomachs.

I had some opportunity to read the book in the next day or so, but word soon came that we had to move on. I found the guard who had taken me to the wood-chopping and explained that I had borrowed a book and would like to return it. To my disappointment, he would not take me but promised to return it himself and I do not doubt he did for she was an attractive woman. I have told this story to illustrate that even when this European conflict was nearing its close some veneer of civilastion remained.

After our days of rest, we had three days when we covered about fifteen miles each day and reached the River Elbe at Junker Wehnigen which I have been unable to find on a map. Crossing the bridge I reflected how exciting it would have been and how I would have appreciated it in other circumstances, to have walked from near the Vistula across the Oder to the Elbe, previously just wiggly lines on a map.

The weather was now spring-like and we walked along optimistically as we were heading westwards. We had heard from another column of British POWs who had a secret wireless set that the Americans had crossed the Rhine. It was now quite easy to leave our billets at night and visit neighbouring villages, though sometimes we were turned away or received no answer. In spite of this I remember one pleasant evening when I was invited in for coffee and cakes and spent a happy time discussing the progress of the war with an atlas to explain where we were in relation to the reported position of the Allied forces. The chief concern of my hosts was that the American or British should reach them earlier than the Russians.

This was the latter part of March and we passed through Dannenburg, Velzen and Enschede. Food issues from the Germans had become irregular, so for the first time since the black days of 1940, food became an obsession and almost the sole subject of conversation. Everyone would talk about pre-war parties and the food they would have when they reached home. I remember one morning, I day-dreamed about buying a new cottage loaf and a chunk of cheese and eating it all in a sitting.

On these last days of marching, we passed a number of burnt-out railway wagons, the result of Allied bombing, although we had not experienced any raids on our route. We found some wagons which had contained sugar and we helped ourselves to some of this which had just been scorched. We also found and tried some raw swedes, but these were less palatable.

So on 27th. March 1945, we came to Celle where to our astonishment after trekking some 900 kilometres, we were told that we were being taken by train to a permanent camp on the Lüneberger Heide. We were issued with a bread ration for the journey and the next day climbed into the inevitable cattle trucks. However the doors were not shut as on that terrible 48 hour journey in 1940 from Trier to Thorn, nor were we so crowded. We travelled from Celle via Lehrte to Hildesheim but had to stay in the wagon except for calls of nature. Next day the train took us to Emmerke - and then back to Hildesheim. It was not until Good Friday, 30th. March, that we were allowed to leave the train at Hildesheim where we were to go into a camp.

We were not averse to this as we had survived in camps for nearly five years with varying degrees of comfort. There was always an issue of food, eatable if not adequate or exciting, and there was a roof over our heads, and water. We all felt the war was nearly over as the Allies were advancing. After Saturday and Sunday however we were not so happy. We were once again sleeping on straw; our daily food ration was a spoonful of watery soup without taste, and a tenth portion of a two-pound loaf. This was quite inadequate and we were also now guarded inside a compound there was no opportunity to barter.

Some, including my friend John Wilkinson, went out to work on the Tuesday. They reported that the town had been heavily bombed and that they had been repairing damaged railway tracks. John suggested that I should join him at work on the Wednesday and seize any opportunity to escape. After the first two days of being a prisoner, I had not seriously considered escaping as I thought the

chance of success too remote. Now however it seemed the right thing to do as it was rumoured the Allies were only about seventy five miles away to the south and west, so I agreed, but insisted that Thomo should be offered the chance to join us.

John was not too keen as he and I were young and single, whereas Thomo was older with two children. Anyway Thomo declined the chance, so John and I left most of our possessions behind, went to work in our battle dress with just a small haversack each to carry the most useful things and would not call for comment if searched.

Our opportunity came quickly on that Wednesday morning. We were fortunate enough to be in a gang of twenty working under two guards at the furthest point of any British prisoners from the town. We had been told we would be taken to a shelter as soon as an air-raid warning was sounded, though no one really knew of its whereabouts. The siren did sound after we had been at work only a few minutes, so seizing our oppotunity, John and I, mixed hurriedly with a crowd of all nationalities making their way from the town. In the confusion, when the others turned in one direction we walked confidently the other way on the road leading to the countryside. We never saw our guards again.

We met an Estonian from whose halting German we tried to glean the local geography, without success. Taking our direction from the sun, we followed a track leading uphill westwards through some woods. We encountered a French prisoner too scared of associating with escapees to help us. I shall not forget that initial taste of freedom, with the dew still on the grass, wild flowers in the clearings and the sun climbing into the heavens. I thought the air which I breathed was fresher and purer.

In the middle of the wood, we came upon a barbed wire compound where our track met a road. As we passed it we noticed a German NCO at the entrance, so in accordance with a pre-arranged plan, I asked him for some coffee, saying that we had lost our comrades with whom we had marched from Poland. He was sorry to be unable help but all the Poles he was guarding were out working. We discussed the war and the possibility of an early end, then he volunteered the information that the Americans were advancing and would soon be here. We expressed ignorance of this and took care not to display too great a belief. We parted on the best of terms with mutual expressions of goodwill.

The meeting gave us confidence that we could outwit any German, so when we came out of the wood at the outskirts of a village, we decided to seek food and drink there. At the first house the outraged woman slammed the door in our faces, leaving her child however to the mercy of her unwelcome viusitors. At the next, we were more fortunate and were given cakes, apples and coffee, as well as advice to avoid passing through the village by taking a short cut across the fields to the next main road.

We gratefully followed this aadvice and presently came to a crosstroads, across which a German army staff car was being driven. We decided to ignore it, but the car stopped and an officer called us over. He asked us who we were and where we were going. With a polite salute I told him the same story as before, which we supported by showing our POW number discs. The tale was accepted if not fully believed. We were directed to turn south at the crossroads as no one was allowed to continue westwards. We were delighted - not only had we bamboozled an officer, but if the roads were blocked to the west, the Allies must be near!

Our self-esteem was soon shaken. When it started to rain, we looked for food and shelter at the first of a row of cottages. We were asked to wait by a woman whilst another slipped out to return with a man who took us into a nearby factory from where we were fetched by a policeman - a typical fat musical comedy village policeman. Up till then we could have got away at any time, but having given a story we had not wished to weaken it by starting a hue and cry. Now we were sunk!

We were quite impressed by the cleanliness of the cell at the local police station, and by the bowls of cabbage and potato stew. Unfortunately it was 24 hours later before the next food arrived - more bowls of cabbage soup.

We spent a not uncomfortable night on the wooden benches in the cell, and after much banging on the door, we were allowed to wash and empty the toilet bucket. We had hoped in vain that the police would produce coffee and bread, but we were merely locked in again. Later we heard the air raid siren and the sound of heavy feet leaving the building for shelter. An eerie silence followed for a time, then the 'all clear'. Obviously the police thought we were expendable.

When the policemen brought our soup at midday, we heard that a soldier was to take us to another camp for the British; we were not at all worried as long as we did not have to return to Hildesheim.

When the German came to collect us, we marched to a railway station and travelled by train, but unfortunately in a south-eastward direction. We arrived in the evening of 5th. April at a typical camp of hutments beside the railway line occupied by prisoners who had been marched from Silesia. We were allocated bunks.

Next morning we found their rations were bad and were supplemented with potatoes from nearby fields and fat black slugs which they collected from the hills. Happily we had no time to sample these as next afternoon, the order was given for all to be prepared once more to march - eastwards of course. It is one thing to walk six hundred miles towards home, and another to retrace one's steps, so we sneaked out of the camp into some railway sheds and hid in a coal bunker until night fall.

When we judged that all was clear we returned to the camp and hid under beds in one room. It was as well we did, as before long a soldier passed the window looking for missing prisoners. Fortunately he did not enter to search the hut. We remained uncomfortably concealed until we judged the danger was past. We found that others had had the same idea as about twelve to twenty men emerged in twos and threes from various rooms of the huts.

We unearthed hidden sacks of potatoes, made fires and baked, boiled and roasted them until we were replete. We settled down, carefully concealed, to sleep.

As soon as it was light, we quit the camp. I carried a can of cold potatoes and John one of cold coffee. We crossed a bridge and were once again on a road going west. We met some civilians and a soldier, and wished them good-day. Our confidence returned, but once again it was short-lived.

A motor cycle stopped nar us, and the rider (who we learned was a railway policeman) accused us of being escaped prisoners. We denied this accusation indignantly, and once again I told the tale of having lost our comrades from Poland. This time it was openly disbelieved. Apparently some forty of the several hundred in the camp we had left had decided against a further march, and round-up was in progress. "Report at the inn straight down the road, or it will be the worse for you", was the motor cyclist's parting shot. "What do we do now ?" I asked John. "Take the first chance to get off the road", he replied and this we did as fast as possible. No longer could we be innocent lost sheep. We really were on the run!

We followed a track which led us parallel to the main road through empty fields until we came to a road where we saw groups of German soldiers. Opposite our path and the intersection of this road lay some allotments, so we boldly crossed into these and continued our walk past civilians who stopped their digging to stare curiously at two untidy khaki-clad figures still carrying cans.

We came to a wood and nearly bumped into a party of Hiler Youth practising military manoeuvres. This meant making a wide detour, for these youngsters might have shot us on sight. We met some French POWs who were expecting to be marched away as they had heard the Allies were near. We came in sight of another road with guards at roadblocks at intervals and we saw they were stopping all passers-by. Once again we were on a track which met the road between the guarded road blocks with another path opposite leading through some fields to a farm. We strode confidently up the road, but just as we were about to cross a German soldier, obviously a sentry, bobbed up with a rifle.

"Where are you going " he challenged. "Only to the village up there", I replied, flourishing my can of potatoes. Before he could dispute it, we carried on up the hill without a backward glance. As we neared the top, we saw that a ploughman had stopped and was waiting for us. There could be no going back to face the sentry; we had to meet the ploughman. He however was a Pole who with a Dutchman was working the farm for a German. He told us that the Americans must be near as the French prisoners on a nearby farm had been marched off that morning.

There was only one thing to do - hide. We asked for suggestions. Only a shed filled with dusty and verminous potato straw was available, so we crawled in there. Later the Pole and the Dutchman visited us and promised to bring food next day. We awoke next morning and discussed our next move. It was Sunday, 8th. April, and John's birthday. He would have liked to celebrate by completing our escape, but suddenly flashes appeared in a small town, Einbeck, we had by-passed the day before. We soon realised that shells were being fired to our west and that we were in 'no-man's land'.

The shelling continued until evening, and when darkness and silence fell, I had to dissuade John from investigating. Next morning, (9th.April) we followed a track leading south to a village and stopped at the first house, resolved to try our luck. We asked if we could have some milk and were given some. They looked scared and told us the Americans were in the village.

Hastily leaving the house, we hurried down the road to the village pub and to the jeep which stood outside. The driver asked us who we were. We replied, British prisoners-of-war. "Oh yeah", he said mildly interested, "how long were you in ?" "Five years", we said. His jaw dropped, no longer disinterested. "Five years", he gasped. He reported to one of his officers and soon we were surrounded by a crowd anxious to shower us with food and cigarettes.

John and I shook hands solomnly. We had made it! We were FREE.

References

1. QVR. = Queen Victoria Rifles
2. KRR. = Kings Royal Rifles
3. "Red Cap" = Military Police
4. Fifth Columnist = A traitor or spy in contact with the enemy
5. Lüneberger Heide = This was where Montgomery took the German surrender.